Stay Strong:

A Musician's Journey from Congo

Published by Clockwise Press Inc., 201 Taylor Mills Drive North, Richmond Hill, Ontario, L4C 2T5

www.clockwisepress.com

christie@clockwisepress.com   solange@clockwisepress.com

10 9 8 7 6 5 4 3 2 1

Library and Archives Canada Cataloguing in Publication

Hyde, Natalie, 1963-, author

Stay strong : a musician's journey from Congo / Natalie Hyde. (Arrivals ; 1)

Issued in print and electronic formats.

ISBN 978-0-9939351-2-1 (paperback)
ISBN 978-0-9939351-3-8 (html)

1. Misigaro, Gentil. 2. Musicians--Canada--Biography--Juvenile literature. 3. Immigrants--Canada--Biography--Juvenile literature. 4. Congolese--Canada--Juvenile literature.

I. Title.

ML3930.M678H98 2015   j780'.92   C2015-904250-
XC2015-904251-8

The text in this book uses OpenDyslexic and Impact typefaces.
Cover image and maps courtesy of iStock Images
Back cover photo courtesy of Roger Montes
Book design by CommTech Unlimited
Printed in Canada by Webcom

Stay Strong:

A Musician's Journey from Congo

Natalie Hyde

CLOCKWISE
PRESS

For my mother, who knows firsthand the sorrows and joys of leaving one country to make a home in another.

Table of Contents

Foreword

Everyone is born equal. Just as no one chooses his or her own family, clan, tribe, country, continent, or race, no one chooses to be a refugee. I've come to understand that anyone can be a refugee, a newcomer, an immigrant, and a foreigner! All those names are just a reality of life. The difference comes from how we choose to live our lives and how we treat each other as human beings. We are all capable of making a difference in our world regardless of age, race, gender, or religion. If we can learn to build unity like how God intended it, no one would feel like a guest or a stranger in their own world!

I've come to realize that humankind builds unity in sameness instead of building unity out of diversity and in our differences.

It is not easy to be an immigrant or a newcomer in any place, adapting to a new culture, new weather, new ways of life, and new languages. Starting from zero can be frustrating and discouraging, and sometimes dreams start to die.

But through my experiences as someone who had to start from zero many times as a newcomer,

I can say that every person has something to give, to share, and to do for somebody else! It can be material things, acts of kindness, talking to somebody and asking them how they are doing, or just letting someone know that you care—it can change a life. Canadians are blessed to have this amazing country; we should always be grateful for the gift of being in this nation. And as we do so, we should also remember to think about other people as well—whether that's our neighbours or people across the continent or across the world.

My parents taught me three things, which have shaped the way I live as a person: "It is more blessed to give than to receive," "Do all you can to live in peace with everyone," and "Love conquers everything." As I conclude, it's important to remember that anyone can make our world a better place by starting with one life at a time!

—Gentil Misigaro

Preface

Canada is a nation of immigrants. Our ancestors came from all over the world to settle here and call this country home. Immigrants have played important yet often overlooked roles in this nation's history. They built railroads, mined for gold, farmed the prairies, fished the coastal waters, and started businesses that drove Canada's economy. Even today, immigrants bring to Canada a wealth of skills, knowledge, and talent.

Stay Strong is the story of one such immigrant. In 2010 Gentil Misigaro and his family were welcomed to Canada as war-affected refugees originally from the Democratic Republic of Congo. His story is one of determination and hope in the face of grave danger, hate, and loss.

Although much of the dialogue in the book is quoted directly from interviews with Gentil Misigaro, some has been recreated based on the oral history provided to improve context and narrative flow.

Prologue

Gentil Misigaro felt the wheels of the plane hit the ground with a bump. They had arrived. It had already been an exhausting trip from Kampala, Uganda, to Toronto, Ontario, but he forgot his tiredness with the realization that he was in Canada.

"Are we there?" his brother David asked him, peering out the plane window.

"We're in Canada, but we're not home yet."

David sat back in his seat. "I like the sound of that—home. But how much longer do we have to travel?"

"One more flight," Gentil told him. "We are going to Winnipeg in Manitoba."

"Can't we go by car? I'm tired of flying."

"I think it would be a long drive because the flight is two and a half hours."

"Oh," David said. "It sure is taking a long time to reach home."

"I know, but we're on Canadian soil now—our new country."

It felt good to call Canada his country, and

now that they were here Gentil knew that one chapter of his life had closed and another had begun.

As they taxied to the terminal, Gentil looked through the small plane window to get his first glimpse of his new home. It looked so different from the place he had left. The vibrant greens, browns, and oranges of Africa had been replaced with the whites, greys, and silvers of Canada. It looked cold and icy. But Gentil didn't mind. They were the colours of a new beginning. They were the colours of hope.

1

G entil watched as what seemed like his entire village packed up and left. Magunga was hilly and lush with trees and grasses, which were good for raising cattle and crops. But the round huts with reed roofs that dotted the hillside were soon to be empty as sixty-eight people left for the border to escape the horrors that were heading their way. Only six years old, Gentil was already used to running into the bush to hide whenever the army would descend on his village.

Gentil's tribe, the Banyamulenge, had become a target for rebels and the national army alike. They were descended from the Tutsi tribe in neighbouring Rwanda. Many generations ago, their ancestors had settled in Congo but many Congolese still considered them outsiders. In Rwanda, the remaining Tutsis had been targeted by the majority Hutu tribe. Hundreds of thousands of Tutsis had been slaughtered in a racially motivated war.

With this genocide barely over in Rwanda, the conflict seemed to have crossed the border into Gentil's home country, which they called Zaire (now called the Democratic Republic of Congo). Thefts and beatings had escalated to killings and kidnappings. Everyone in Gentil's home village of Magunga was afraid, and they knew they had to leave or die.

The quickest route to safety was to head straight to Lake Tanganyika, which was about a day's walk away, and then take a boat up the lake to the town of Uvira. There they would cross the borders into either Rwanda or Burundi. The longer and more dangerous route was travelling over land to Uvira where rebels had many miles to hide in the forests and bushes, waiting to ambush unsuspecting refugees. No one wanted to risk walking the whole way.

The villagers gathered their belongings and with hugs and good wishes began their trek to the lake and the relative safety of a new country. Gentil's family didn't go with them; they had to stay behind. His mother had sold their cows for the much-needed money, which would be used to buy or bribe their way out of the country. But the money hadn't arrived. They had to wait.

Gentil took this time to visit his grandparents.

They weren't coming...the trip would not be possible at their age, so they would have to take their chances and stay.

"Don't be afraid, Gentil," his grandfather told him. "I have been praying for you. I know that you and your family will make it and you will survive. Gentil, you will be like a light to the family and change the world."

Gentil felt a great sense of relief at his words. His grandfather was a man of strong faith, and if he believed Gentil would be okay, then he thought it must be true.

As evening fell, Gentil heard the sound of someone running toward the village. His mother hurried out of their hut with a worried look on her face. Who was coming? Gentil got ready to grab his brother Reagan's hand and run into the bush.

"I have news! I have news!" a voice called as a man came into view.

He stopped running at the edge of the village and bent over to catch his breath.

"What is it?" Gentil's mother asked him.

"They're dead," he said, choking up with emotion. "They're all dead!"

"Who's dead?"

"Everyone. Everyone who left this morning. Their boat was attacked on the lake. They drowned."

"Are you sure?" Gentil's uncle Jean de Dieux asked, coming over. "Are you sure it was the same boat?"

The man nodded, a look of horror on his face as he relived what he had witnessed.

"Everyone?" Gentil's mother asked, almost in a whisper.

"Someone said they saw two men bobbing in the water and that a fishing boat was going to rescue them, if they got there in time." The man wiped his eyes. "But only two."

No one spoke as the enormity of what happened sank in—practically an entire village wiped out in a matter of hours.

"Don't go on the lake," the man said. "Find another way through the countryside. The lake is a route to certain death."

The news hit Gentil's family hard. Everyone from the village was a friend, neighbour, or relative. Gentil was suddenly grateful that the cow money hadn't arrived the day before. If he and his family had left with the others, they would be dead now, too.

Night fell, but Gentil couldn't sleep; the quiet of the village was eerie. He kept waiting to hear the shouts of attackers and the blast of gunfire. He was sure that the army or the rebels would capture them before morning. Every snap of a twig or rustle of grass made his heart race. He was exhausted by the time the sky began to lighten, but they had survived the night.

Morning came and there was a flurry of activity. The money from the cows had come and they could leave. Gentil's father had already gone to Rwanda a few months earlier to secure a job and a place for them to stay, so Gentil, his mother, Miriam, younger brother, Reagan, and his uncle Jean De Dieux stuffed their clothes, some food, blankets, and cooking utensils into bags.

"No, not the guitar," his mother told him, knowing that Gentil wanted to take it with them. His father had taught him to play and the only thing Gentil loved more than hearing his father's music was trying to play it himself.

"But we can't leave it," Gentil said.

"It's too big and bulky."

"I'll carry it myself."

"It will slow us down and put everyone at risk."

Gentil reluctantly left it.

They said a hurried goodbye to those staying behind, mostly the elderly who couldn't make the trip, and started off in the opposite direction the main group had taken the day before. They were going to attempt the long and arduous journey over land to Uvira.

Travel was slow. Their bags were heavy and they had to take small roads and trails to avoid being seen. After they had been walking for about fourteen hours, they finally spotted the village of Akuku.

"Where are we going to sleep tonight?" Gentil asked, seeing the sun lowering on the horizon. His legs were sore, his arms ached, and his stomach rumbled. They had barely rested and hadn't eaten all day.

"We'll find somewhere," his mother said. "Someone will share their home with us."

Although they looked a bit nervous, the villagers of Akuku welcomed them. The villagers knew that simply by harbouring this targeted Banyamulenge tribe, they were putting themselves in danger. But Congo has a culture of helping and sharing, and these people were willing to risk their own safety in order to help a group in such a desperate situation.

Gentil's mother took some sweet potatoes, cassava, and plantains from their bags and helped their hosts make supper. They all sat down together for ugali—a mash of cooked cassava—and spicy vegetable stew. Gentil wolfed down his food.

"What are your plans?" one villager asked Jean de Dieux as they finished eating.

"We are heading north tomorrow, towards Uvira."

"I heard two villages northeast of here were attacked last night," another villager said.

"What happened?" Jean de Dieux asked.

"Seven families were butchered. The rest fled into the bush," he replied. A silence fell over the group. "They say it was the rebels."

"If I were you, I wouldn't go that way. The rebels are probably still in the area. You should go west and then north to circle around the danger," another man told Jean de Dieux.

"But that will take us farther away from Uvira, not closer, and add at least two days to our journey."

"Better two more days than dead in a ditch," the villager said.

"Didn't the army do anything to protect the villagers?" Gentil's mother asked.

One man made a dismissive sound. "The army cannot be trusted, either. I heard that they are taking all able-bodied men they come across as recruits. Men with farms, families, jobs. Doesn't matter, they take anyone."

To Gentil, it felt like an icy breeze raced

down his spine. It was the same feeling he had the night his father told him he was leaving for Rwanda. It was a mixture of dread and sadness. Gentil wondered if his father knew that they were on their way. Had he heard about the gangs of rebels ransacking entire villages and slaughtering people without fear of punishment?

No one slept well, except for Reagan, who, at two years old, was too young to feel the fear that hung around them like a shroud. As soon as the sky lightened, they packed their belongings back in their bags, thanked their hosts, and started walking again.

They had to walk quickly, knowing that their enemies were on the move and waiting for an opportunity to ambush them. Any open space made those on foot vulnerable, so when Gentil heard the sound of the rushing water of the Mutambala River, he approached it with fear. This was a known site of many killings because snipers could hide in the thick jungle on either bank. The bridge consisted of two long poles lined with rough planks spanning the water spilling over treacherous rocks. There were gaps in the planks and no railing at all. One wrong step and someone would be swept away down the raging river.

"Stay beside me," Jean de Dieux said. There

was only room for two people to walk side by side. Gentil's mother had Reagan by the hand ahead of them.

Gentil stepped carefully, trying not to get a foot wedged in the gaps or lose his balance.

"But quickly," Jean de Dieux added. "We are too exposed here."

A crack of a branch made them freeze. Was it someone with a gun waiting to take a shot?

"Hurry!"

Gentil tried to go faster but his foot slipped. He tripped and started to go over the side.

"I got you," Jean de Dieux said, grabbing his arm at the last second.

As soon as the group set foot on the other side, they hurried to take cover in the forest. There was no time for Gentil to reflect on how close he had just come to death; they had to move on.

That night was another village, another shared meal, and another restless sleep. Leaving at first light for their brutally long hike was difficult. Walking all day and eating only one meal at night was taking its toll. On the third day, Gentil's bag felt as if it were filled with rocks. No one had much strength left, so the family started shedding non-essentials, just leaving them behind on the side of the road. Clothes, food, extra pots—everything was scrutinized for its necessity, and if it seemed as if they could live without it, out it went.

Gentil, who was struggling to carry anything at all because he was so weak and tired, was given the task of carrying just a blanket, but even that felt like an immense burden for his arms.

"I don't think I can," he told his mother. "It's too heavy."

"We need a blanket, Gentil," she said. "It's cold and raining. You don't have to carry anything else but keep the blanket."

It was the beginning of the rainy season and the rains made everything and everyone damp and cold. In the end, Gentil lugged the blanket, although it seemed to cost him his last bit of energy.

Ahead of them rose the Itombwe Massif. This mountain range runs along the western shore of Lake Tanganyika. The mountains form a plateau that contains the dark and forbidding Itombwe forest and then drop off sharply down to the plain beside the lake. Travelling for a day and a half through foliage so thick they could only see ahead a few metres was nerve wracking. There, they had to worry not only about human predators, but also about poisonous snakes, charging elephants, and territorial gorillas.

Gentil practically collapsed when they found shelter that night. Fear had drained him of strength; he was tired, cold, and weak. He dropped his bags and wished that if he had to lug something bulky and heavy, it had been the guitar. He missed the music that surrounded him back home; it reminded him of happier times with everyone together. He would often hear singing as women did the laundry or men worked in the fields. He tried to remember the sound of it to give him the bit of energy he needed to continue on.

2

Once they were through the forest, the days started blending together and it seemed to Gentil as if they had been walking forever. Some villages were welcoming, but others refused to let them stay; the fear of retribution was too great. Sometimes they had to go back the way they had just come in order to avoid trouble spots where they heard attackers could be waiting for them.

Just as Gentil thought they must have been nearing the end of their walk, they faced a huge mountain that locals called Kafinda. Temperatures on the mountain were cool during the day and could drop to freezing overnight, leaving frost on the ground. Other people attempting to cross it had succumbed to hypothermia and died. Gentil understood now the importance of the blanket he was still dragging along.

They were on the mountain for a day and a half, shivering and slipping on the slick, steep paths. Relief came when they finally made their way over the top and down the slope on the other side and saw the city of Uvira spread out below them. The city was long and narrow and stretched along the western shore of Lake Tanganyika, which they could see glistening in the sunlight beyond the buildings. At the tip of the lake, the city sat on the border with Burundi. The trip to that border town, which should have only taken a few hours by car from their village, had taken almost a week of solid walking.

"We made it!" Gentil said, so excited to be near the border that he forgot how tired he was.

"We haven't made it yet," Jean de Dieux told him. "Now comes the hardest part."

The hardest part? Gentil thought that walking for miles through the countryside, terrified that at any moment they would be attacked by rebels or predatory animals and then almost freezing to death on a steep mountain crossing were the most dangerous parts of the journey.

"All we have to do is get to the border, don't we?"

"We're not crossing here," Gentil's mother told him. "We are going to Rwanda, and the only way to get there is to travel through Uvira and along the busy road north where we are exposed."

"Why don't we just go through the bush like

before?" Gentil asked. He didn't really want to walk another step, but it sounded safer than going along a crowded road with nowhere to hide.

"It is impossible to walk to the border because of the mountains," Jean de Dieux broke in. "We need to hire a car. It's safer, but it will cost us. How much money do we have?"

The cow money had been carefully guarded the whole trip because they knew it would be needed not only to pay for supplies, but to bribe people. Officials, soldiers, rebels, guards—they all would expect payment. If the family was robbed on the way, there was no way they would make it across the border; that was certain. They had already heard the stories of border guards demanding cash and stripping the refugees of any possessions. The prospect was grim because even if the families made it across after that, they were penniless with no hope of buying food or paying for shelter. But they would worry about that later.

Gentil's mother knew that they could easily lose all their cash, so she did something clever. Banking on the fact that the guards often overlooked the children, she kept some of the family wealth in gold nuggets, which she sewed into the waistband of Gentil's shorts, hoping they would never be found there. Even though some officials stole clothing right off people's backs, surely they would not want a six-year-old's shorts.

If was risky, though. If anyone discovered them trying to hide valuables, the entire family would almost certainly be killed. Gentil tried not to think about it.

The family was thankful when they finally arrived in Uvira because Gentil's mother knew a pastor named Mudakiwa there who would shelter them until they could make arrangements for a car. For three days the family hid in his house, afraid to show their faces outside. The pastor finally found a man who was willing to drive them north to the border of Rwanda. He would have to be well paid, though, because he was putting himself in grave danger if they were caught.

"Wake up, Gentil," his mother said, shaking him. "We have to leave now."

It was dark outside when Gentil and his family left the house. It was too dangerous for them to go out during the day, so they said their goodbyes and thanked the pastor under the cover of darkness.

"Wait, there are already people in this van," Gentil said to his uncle, noticing some women sitting in the seats.

"It's okay," Jean de Dieux told him. "They are

the driver's family. They will sit by the windows so when anyone looks, they will only see a man driving some ladies to go shopping or to work. We will need to stay low and hidden."

It was uncomfortable to be squished down beside Reagan by everyone's feet in the mini-van for the hot, bumpy car ride, but it was a relief not to have to walk for a while. It was a slow ride through what sounded like a lot of traffic. Gentil felt dizzy. When you can't see where you're going, you can't anticipate which way to move and you get tossed around a lot. Suddenly, the driver slammed on the brakes. Gentil and Reagan collided into the seat in front of them.

"It's a roadblock," the driver whispered. "Stay down! Stay down!"

Gentil could hear the shouts of soldiers coming closer and his heart raced. He crouched down as small as he could. The driver opened his door and got out to speak to the guards so they wouldn't come too close to the van, but it didn't work—suddenly the doors flung open.

"Get out! Get out!" the soldiers yelled, pointing their guns inside the van.

Everyone scrambled out. The ladies stood by the side of the van, and Gentil and Reagan huddled beside their mother. The guards were yelling and waving their guns. Every time the barrel was pointed at him, Gentil flinched. He could see the guard's finger on the trigger and with all the commotion, he was terrified that the gun would go off and kill him.

The driver tried to talk to the agitated soldiers. After a few minutes of tense negotiations, he came over to them.

"If you pay them, they will let you go."

"But we won't have enough money for the border!" Gentil's mother said.

"You won't make it to the border at all if you don't pay them," the driver told her, looking over his shoulder nervously. "Now, quickly, before they change their minds and shoot us all."

Gentil's mother handed over the money and he and his family moved back toward the van. The soldiers continued yelling insults at them but let them go.

They were badly shaken, but grateful they could continue. The famiy climbed back in and once the guards were out of sight, they crouched down again. Gentil could hear from the noise that the streets were crowded with people, motorbikes, and cars. It was slow going. Gentil prayed that they would not be stopped again.

No such luck.

Roadblocks were everywhere. Soldiers had been alerted to the trick of hiding refugees in vans and cars. Gentil and his family were dragged out of the mini-van several more times. Each time, Gentil was sure the rifles would be turned on them, but somehow Jean de Dieux and the driver managed to plead, bribe, and beg for their lives. As the van pulled away from these stops, those on the streets began stoning the vehicle. The sound of rocks bouncing off the metal sides terrified Gentil. Reagan started to cry. Gentil's mother held him close.

After many hours of roadblocks, yelling, and more stones bouncing off the van, they finally approached the border between Zaire and Rwanda near the village of Kamanyola.

"Good luck," the driver said, letting them out along the road that led to the border. Gentil's mother paid him and thanked him. He climbed quickly back into the van and drove off back to Uvira.

Gentil and his family walked down the road until they saw the border guards. Across that imaginary line on the road was what they hoped was a safer, more peaceful life. But first they had to get across. They had heard the stories of the brutality of the border guards. If the guards didn't get what they considered enough payment, the word was that they would kill the refugees without a second thought and throw their bodies in the ditch.

Gentil kept thinking of the gold nuggets hidden in his shorts. What would they do to him if they found them?

When it was their turn to approach the border guards, Jean de Dieux handed over all the money they had left, praying it would be enough. The guards took it, counted it, and then looked over the group carefully, as if they wanted more. One of the guards started patting down Jean de Dieux and asking his mother to show him there was nothing hidden on her. Next he stood in front of Gentil. Gentil stood still.

The guard looked him up and down and for a second Gentil thought he was going to move away, but then the guard seemed to look twice at his shorts. He came closer, and Gentil's breath caught in his throat. He didn't dare look at his mother.

The guard checked his pockets and then the hem of his shorts. Any second now his hands would press on Gentil's waistband and find the gold. And then it would be over.

But the guard seemed satisfied and moved away—he hadn't noticed the lumpy waistband.

Gentil tried not to make his shaking obvious; he could finally breathe again.

They still weren't being let through, though; they were told to stand at the side of the road. A group of refugees who had been searched, including Gentil's family, stood huddled together waiting for permission to cross. Gentil realized that many of them were Rwandans who had fled into Congo during the genocide in Rwanda and were now trying to go home.

In the milling crowd, Gentil heard his mother gasp.

"Jacques! Jacques, is that you?" she called.

A young man ran over and embraced her. Gentil could hardly believe it; it was his mother's brother. Another uncle had found them.

There was suddenly a lot of yelling between the two groups of guards. The Rwandan guards down the road were growing impatient. They wanted their citizens to be allowed to return home. They threatened to start a fight with the Congolese guards if the refugees weren't allowed to cross immediately. Gentil huddled close to his mother. If fighting broke out between the two sides, they would be caught in the crossfire.

Not wanting to get into a fight at that time, the Congolese guards decided to let the group waiting on the side of the road go. Relief washed over all of them as they were waved through. A few minutes' walk down the road and they were in Rwanda.

"Grandfather said we'd make it," Gentil said. "Now everything will be okay."

Jean de Dieux and Jacques exchanged looks.

"We have nothing to our names," Jean de Dieux said. "No clothes, no pots, and no food."

"And nowhere to live," Jacques added.

Gentil felt the nuggets in his waistband.

"But we can buy all that. At least we won't be attacked in our sleep."

Gentil's mother put an arm around his shoulder.

"That's right," she said. "We have lost everything except hope."

3

It seemed strange to Gentil that simply by walking down a dirt road he would be in another country and could feel so much safer. The feeling wouldn't last for too long, though. The reality of being a refugee in a foreign country was about to become apparent.

The Rwandan guards gathered all the refugees into in a big group, just past the border.

"Do we have to start walking again?" Gentil asked, not seeing a village or town anywhere. All he could see were bushes.

"We're going to a refugee camp," his mother told him.

Gentil had heard people mention these camps before, but he had never seen one.

"Is it like Magunga?"

"No. We will live in a tent surrounded by lots and lots of other tents with all the other refugees until we can find your father and get settled again."

"How far away is it?"

"I don't know," she said.

At first, Gentil was delighted when trucks with big trailers pulled up—no more walking! Then the guards started cramming them into the trailers like cattle. Gentil tried hard to keep some elbowroom for himself and Reagan, but the guards seemed to want to pack in as many people as possible.

"I can't breathe!" Reagan said. People were pressing into both the boys from all sides.

"Stay by me," Gentil told him, trying to not let the crush of people separate them.

"They are going to be suffocated," Jean de Dieux said to Jacques. "Quick, lean over them like this."

Jean de Dieux stood in front of Gentil and braced himself on the outside wall, making a protective space over him so others wouldn't crush his small nephew.

They stayed in that position for the entire journey. It was a difficult enough way to travel for a short distance, but this trip lasted for hours over roads that, thanks to years of civil war, were rutted and full of potholes.

Some people couldn't take the claustrophobic surroundings and begged to be let off. Seeing that the trucks weren't stopping for anyone, these desperate people either jumped out or had others push them out.

When the trucks finally stopped, people scrambled out of them, gulping the fresh air. Gentil's legs were cramped and wobbly, and Reagan had to be carried out by Jacques. Gentil's mother, who had been squashed against the truck wall for hours, was bruised and sore. They thought that walking for hours every day had been hard, but this truck ride was much harder.

They had arrived at a United Nations refugee camp. What was spread out before them was a sea of tents that looked like a field of blue, green, and white termite mounds. The smoke from small fires drifted upwards out of the sea of mud. It was a depressing sight compared to the beautiful green hills they had left behind, but at least here they would be safe. After registering, they were given a saucepan, blankets, a small ration of maize, and a tent.

Conditions in the camp were crowded and Gentil's family had to walk a long way to find a spot for their tent. With the payments and bribes to cross the border, most people had nothing left with which to start over. Gentil's family was only a little luckier...they had the hidden gold. They still had to be careful, though. With so many desperate people in the camp, they could become a target for thieves if anyone found out about the gold.

Conditions were so bad that Gentil and his family stayed only three days in the border camp. As quickly as they could, they headed toward Rwanda's capital city, Kigali. They needed to find Gentil's father. Did he know they were alive? How would they even begin to look for him?

They hoped to have better luck at a different refugee camp closer to the capital.

When they arrived at the new camp, they went through the process of getting a tent and some supplies and setting up their makeshift shelter for a second time.

"Are you Miriam, Gentil, and Reagan?" an aid worker asked Gentil's mother as she registered.

"Yes."

"There's someone looking for you. He's been here every day for two weeks checking the camp lists."

Just as she said this, a man came running over to them.

"Miriam!" It was Gentil's father. "I can't believe it!"

Gentil hugged his dad tightly. It had been a long time since their family was together.

"I thought I had lost you all," his father said, holding them close. "They told me everyone had drowned."

"We didn't go with the others," his mother said. "We were waiting for the money from the cows."

"When the news reached me, I thought I had lost my whole family. I was in mourning for a week."

"How did you know how to find us?" Gentil asked.

"One of the two men who survived sent word through his relatives that you were still alive. That's when I started checking the camps. I didn't know where you would cross the border, so I went to all the camps asking if you had registered."

Gentil's father helped them gather their few belongings and took them to Kigali where they moved into a small house he had rented. There they started to piece their lives back together.

Gentil's first action in his new country was to go to school. Education was important to his family and his tribe. But going to school was difficult, not only because his family needed money to pay the fees, but because the journey to school itself was full of danger.

The hope they felt as they crossed the

border into Rwanda for a better life had started to fade as fear once again crept into their lives. Even though the genocide in Rwanda had ended, there were still kidnappings and killings of members of the Tutsi and Banyamulenge tribes. And on top of that, there were landmines left over from the civil war hiding everywhere. The walk to school could be deadly. There were no proper roads or sidewalks to make a safe path to get anywhere. Gentil wasn't sure from day to day which classmates would be there—some didn't make it home the day before. He wasn't sure if he'd make it home, either.

Even at home, the family wasn't safe. Late one night, at about 1 am, there was a pounding at the door.

"Open the door right away or you are all finished!" a voice yelled.

What was going on? It felt to Gentil that they were never free from fear. Even in the middle of the night, someone was threatening them on their doorstep. Rwanda was supposed to be better than Congo.

They tried to remain quiet. Maybe if they didn't speak, the men would just go away.

But the pounding only got louder.

"Open up, now, or we'll shoot!"

Gentil's father moved towards the door.

"No, no!" his mother begged. "Don't open it!"

"If we don't, they'll just break down the door and throw in a grenade, and then we will all die."

"Come on, come on!" the voices yelled.

"I'm coming, I'm coming," his father told them, going to unlock the door.

Two men in soldiers' uniforms burst into the room with their guns drawn. Without hesitating they started beating Gentil's father. With the butt end of his rifle, the one attacker hit him in the head and sent him sprawling to the ground. The rest of the family huddled against the wall, horrified.

"What do you want?" his father asked between blows. "Tell me what you want and I'll give it to you!"

But the two men didn't answer him, they just kept hitting.

Gentil's father had some martial arts training, and as the one attacker tried to hit him with the rifle again, his father grabbed it from him and turned the gun on them.

They backed down immediately.

"Now tell me what you want!" his father demanded.

"We heard there were guns here. We are supposed to check for weapons."

"What good does it do to beat me to death first?" Gentil's father asked. "If you need to check, then check."

His father kept the rifle trained on them as they briefly looked around. It seemed to Gentil that they didn't search very hard and he wondered if that was the real reason for the attack.

When they were done, the one soldier held out his hand for his gun. Everyone tensed. Would the soldier take the gun and shoot them?

But after he got the gun back, the two men left as quickly as they came.

The family stood in stunned silence while listening to the footsteps fade. Within minutes, Gentil and his family packed up a few things and left to spend the night at a friend's house. There was no way they would be able to sleep in their own house that night.

Gentil followed his family in the darkness, wondering if he would ever feel safe—anywhere. The fear that had surrounded him for as long as he could remember had settled in his mind, numbing him. He couldn't think; he couldn't feel. All he could do was go through the motions and hope that someday the fear would loosen its grip. But it didn't look like it would happen here. Here there were hidden landmines, kidnappings, and nighttime attacks. Where would they have to go to find peace and security?

4

Moving. After only a few months in the house in Kigali, they were moving again.

Leaving Congo to move to Rwanda had only given them temporary relief from violence and danger. Now the threat of violence was rearing its ugly head again. They didn't feel safe in the house in Kigali where they were attacked that night. Every time there was a noise, even if something fell off a shelf, the whole family jumped. So once more they gathered their belongings and left.

Gentil's father had finished his training to be a pastor, so this time they moved to an area where he would preach to a small community. They hoped that there they could settle without living in constant fear.

Gentil and his siblings had to start over in another new school, which was difficult, but Gentil knew that the only way to succeed in life was to first get an education. But each time they moved, he had to make new friends and try to fit in with a different curriculum. Each school district had its own way of doing things; there was no common standard for grade levels or subjects.

While Gentil usually caught up quickly in his studies, facing the bullying and discrimination was more difficult. He was picked on for being a refugee, for being from a Tutsi tribe, or for just being new each time he changed schools. But school was so important to him that he persevered, and by the second term, he was usually back at the top of his class. In the ten years his family lived in Rwanda, Gentil went to eleven different schools.

Things were changing at home, too. After a couple of years working as a pastor in Rwanda, Gentil's father welcomed visitors from Germany as part of his pastoring duties. Knowing the family's love of music, one of the German pastors named Manfred Mielke brought them the gift of four guitars. Finally the family could play again!

Now that Gentil was a teenager, his father began to give him more detailed instructions on how to play guitar. Gentil's favourite time was in the evenings after dinner when music once again flowed through their home. Everyone joined in singing and playing; it was the only joy in an otherwise hard life. Music was something that was keeping the family together.

Now that music was back in his life, Gentil hungered to learn more. After practising for a couple of years on the guitars that the Germans had brought, he now turned his sights to the piano.

There was no way to afford lessons, but his father had another idea. He had one of his friends create a musical resource for Gentil: a handmade book that showed the notes for all the different piano chords.

It was like a musical bible. Gentil couldn't put it down. He studied it, memorizing which keys went together to make the different sounds and practising the finger movements on paper. But without an actual keyboard, he could only hear the chords in his mind. He wanted desperately to try them out, but affording a piano was out of the question.

Though Gentil's father brought in enough income for food, shelter, clothing, and school fees, the family was growing larger. Gentil now had five younger siblings: Reagan, Mandela, Console, Gentille, and David.

As well, Gentil's grandparents, who had stayed behind in Congo, had died, leaving four of his father's younger siblings as orphans. His father made the journey back to get them and bring them to live with him and his family in Rwanda. Gentil was especially close to his uncle Fred since they were near in age.

With twelve family members now, space and supplies were stretched thin, but Gentil's desire to broaden his musical skills would not be silenced.

Desperate to try out the chords he had practised in his mind, Gentil headed to the only safe place he knew that had a keyboard—Kirinda Presbyterian Church. The big church was about a hundred years old, as was the organ inside it, and it was only about a fifteen to twenty minute walk away from his home. The only problem was Gentil was in school all day. How would he find time to learn the chords?

Gentil spent every moment he could in the church. In the evenings when there was no service or activities, he got permission to play the organ. Night after night, Gentil snuck away, walking carefully over the ground, watching for unexploded shells and nocturnal predators. Even when he had moved on to high school and boarded there and the walk stretched to 40 minutes, he continued to go. First he practised making the different chords and hearing how the keys sounded together. He had most of them memorized, but this wasn't music. He needed to learn how to put the chords together to make a song.

Gentil asked the people at the church to recommend an instructor. They told him they knew a man named Muswahili in Birambo, a town about two and a half hours away by foot, who could probably help him. Gentil made the long trek to see him even though it took most of the day to get there. A long walk in the hot sun was not going to stop him from mastering the keyboard.

"My name is Gentil, and I'm trying to learn to play the piano," he said. "I heard that you play."

"Well, yes, I play," Muswahili answered, looking a bit uncomfortable.

"Wonderful, because I need someone to teach me. Right now I only know some chords, but I don't know how to make music."

The man shook his head. "I'm sorry, but I'm not a music teacher. I only play a little."

"Well, can you at least show me how these chords go together?"

The man shrugged apologetically. "I'm afraid I can only play in one key. I'm sorry, but I don't think I'll be of much use to you."

Gentil was not giving up that easily—he

had come so far. Maybe if this man could help him understand how and why some chords went together, he could figure the rest out for himself.

"Please, show me. I really want to understand."

"Show you how? I don't have a piano here."

Gentil pulled out a piece of paper and a pencil and drew a rough diagram of the keys on a keyboard. He let the man show him on the drawing where his hands would go for the chords.

"I don't even know their names, but from this chord, I play this one, and then this one."

His fingers touched the lines on the page as Gentil watched every movement carefully.

He thanked the man, and then made the long walk home with the information stored in his memory. When he was at the church that evening, he replayed those chords so he would not forget. Then he looked in his notebook where the chords were all laid out in order. He noticed that the chords that went together for one key were all a certain number of notes away from each other on the scale. So he tried grouping together chords the same count away from each other in another key. It worked. The tiny seed of information that the man had given him had helped him to unlock this mystery.

When he began to play now, the notes and chords began to blend into songs. He made the songs up himself, letting his feelings find their way into his hands and into the music. He wasn't thinking of himself as a composer yet, and he didn't write his songs with the intention of anyone else playing them, or of selling them. They were for himself.

He couldn't get enough of it. He didn't play because he was told to by a music teacher and he didn't practise because it was something he should do to have a career in music. None of those thoughts entered his mind: he played because it felt good. He played through his anger, his frustrations, and his pain because he needed to.

And as he sat alone in the chapel and played and played, he cried. All the sadness, fear, and despair that he had pushed deep down inside of himself in order to survive seemed to be washed away by his tears. The feelings swirled together and then flowed out of him. Relief washed over him and he began to feel again. The music was like medicine, like healing.

5

"**W**here are we going this time?" Gentil asked, packing again. He made sure the guitars were wrapped and ready to go.

"We are going back to Congo," his father said.

"Really? We're going home?"

"Yes, I have been offered a job as a minister in a village not far from where we used to live."

"But isn't it still dangerous?" Gentil asked. He was only six when they left, but he still had nightmares of the long walk and the guards.

"The wars have ended and I think things have settled down," his father said.

During the ten years that the family had lived in Rwanda, two wars had been fought in Congo. Now Rwanda was not as peaceful as they had hoped—there was still so much violence and danger.

The trip back to Congo in 2004 was quick, but even though they were happy to be back in familiar surroundings, Congo had changed. It wasn't as stable as the family had been led to believe and things were about to go downhill again. As an aftermath of the second Congo War, what would become known as the Kivu Conflict erupted with fighting between the Congolese Army and the rebels over control of the valuable mineral resources of Congo.

Gentil and his family had barely been there a month when the situation became critical. The army and the rebels were on the move again.

"Miriam, you have to take the children and go," Gentil's father said.

"But we just got settled." Gentil's mother threw her hands up in the air.

"It's too dangerous here. Both sides of this new fight are looking for recruits. They are even taking children now to become soldiers. Gentil and Fred are at the right age and at risk. You have to leave. Tonight."

"But aren't you coming?"

"I have to finish some work for the church. I'll only be a day or so behind."

"But where should we go? Back to Rwanda? We left there because of the violence!"

"But at least we know people there we can stay with. We can't stay in Congo."

"But how are we going to get there? I can't

walk for a week again." Gentil's mother's eyes filled with tears.

"We can hire a car. If you leave tonight, you should be able to stay ahead of the danger."

Gentil and his family packed. Again. They crammed into a mini-van and took the long ride back to the border in the dark.

His father's decision to stay behind and finish some work was costly. He made it as far as the city of Goma, which sits on the shores of Lake Kivu right across from Rwanda, but with fighting all around and the borders closed, he had to hide out there for seven months.

Back in Rwanda, the family found rooms to rent and Gentil waited for his father to arrive but even there, the militia was hunting down recruits, and he and Fred were still in danger of being kidnapped and forced to join. There was only one thing to do—he and Fred had to flee again. They fled west to Uganda, leaving behind the rest of the family in Rwanda.

Once again Gentil had to move quickly and leave everything behind: family, friends, and possessions, including his beloved musical instruments. At only sixteen years old, it was frightening for Gentil to face the dangers of such a long trip with only his young uncle.

Gentil and Fred had scraped together enough money to hire a car for the journey to Kampala, the capital and largest city in Uganda. Kampala had over one million people—twice as many as there were in Kigali, Rwanda. Rwanda's services, such as hospitals, shops, and public transportation, had been disrupted and even destroyed during its war. But in Uganda, Gentil and Fred hoped they would be able to find medical care, a better education, and the food and supplies they needed.

However, arriving in Uganda was different from arriving in Rwanda. Gentil and his family spoke French, as Congo was once held by the Belgians. French is spoken in Rwanda as well and the culture there is similar to what Gentil knew growing up. In Uganda, on the other hand, the official language is English. And with over thirty different tribes having diverse music, art, and handicrafts, Gentil felt much more like a foreigner here than in Rwanda.

There were social differences as well. Gentil and Fred couldn't even get anyone to direct them to the refugee camp. They arrived in Kampala at ten in the morning and stood in the middle of the busy city until five in the afternoon with no food or money, trying to find out where they needed to go. They tried to stop people on the street to ask directions and while some people said they would take them where they needed to go for a large sum of money, others would ignore them as they passed by. Gentil was brought up to understand that if strangers ask for directions, or food, or help of any kind, you help them, whether or not you know them. In his community back in Congo there was no such thing as homeless people or people going hungry while others ate around them—it was a communal way of living that involved sharing resources. Here, people were too focused on their own troubles to care about those of strangers.

The sun was setting and still Gentil and Fred were stranded and alone.

"Are you looking for something?" a man asked, stopping to speak to them in Swahili, an African language that Gentil could understand.

"Yes, we are trying to find the refugee camp," Gentil said. "We don't know where to go and no one will help us. Can you direct us?"

The man looked them over.

"Where are you from?"

Gentil told him the story of their journey from Congo to Rwanda and back again.

"I know that area of Congo," the man said thoughtfully. "In the 1970s, I was also a refugee.

I was trying to survive the wars in Tanzania, so I fled to Congo, although it was called Zaire back then. I ended up in the region you come from, Sud Kivu, and people were kind to me. I remember what it feels like to be frightened and in a strange country. Until you go through that, you don't know what it's like."

The man nodded to himself. "Let me take you where you need to go."

"But we don't have any money to pay you," Gentil said, remembering how many people had demanded payment before they would help.

"No, I don't want anything. I wish I had money to give to you because you are the ones who need it right now."

Relieved to have found someone kind, the brothers followed the man to the police station. It was protocol that refugees go there first so they could tell the local authorities who they were and make a statement. After that, they had permission to head to the InterAid Uganda office to be registered for the refugee camp, so the man took them there as well. InterAid Uganda is a national humanitarian organization that helps the thousands of displaced persons flooding its borders to find food and shelter.

Gentil was so grateful for this stranger's

help that he wanted to give him something. The man waved him off and went on his way, but to Gentil he was a reminder that the world did have good people in it willing to go out of their way to help someone in need. He thought to himself that if he could ever do the same for a stranger in the future, he would make sure to remember how grateful he felt that day.

Registering with InterAid Uganda was not the end of their troubles. The camps were horribly overcrowded and there just wasn't space left for everyone looking for shelter. They were told that securing a place in the camps took time—about two months—and in that time, those seeking help and protection were on their own.

So even after Gentil and Fred had registered, the boys were forced to find shelter anywhere they could. This was not a pleasant thought; desperate people do desperate things, and at that time Uganda had more refugees than any other country.

"Where are we going to stay tonight?" Fred asked. It was far from safe to spend the night on the streets.

"I don't know and it's getting dark, fast."

"What about a doorway?"

"Too visible," Gentil said.

"How about behind these bushes?" Fred suggested.

"It looks like rain."

They walked down street after street, not even sure where they were anymore.

"This doesn't look like a good area," Fred said.

"No, but look over there."

Fred looked to the empty lot between two buildings where Gentil was pointing. "What?"

"It's an abandoned car," Gentil stated.

They walked over to have a look. The wheels were gone, as was the stereo, steering wheel, and anything else that had any value.

"You're kidding," Fred said.

"It's not a luxury room, but there's a roof overhead if it rains, and if we slouch down in the seats, we're not too obvious."

Fred shrugged. "It's better than walking around all night."

They climbed in and tried to get comfortable. As night fell, sleep eluded them. Every sense was on high alert because every so often they could hear footsteps and shouting. Once, people came so close, Gentil was sure they were going to open the door and find them. He and Fred ducked down so anyone looking in the windows wouldn't see them, and they prayed they would not become the target of bandits who roamed the streets at night looking to steal what they could.

Exhausted, tired, and hungry, they thought that even the crowded camps must be better than this. The morning couldn't come soon enough.

Gentil wondered how and if they would survive two months of this.

6

Gentil wasn't sure what the next day would bring. Had they even made the right choice in going to Uganda? They might avoid being recruited as soldiers, but then again, they might not make it on the streets of Kampala. Gentil remembered the words of his grandfather—he would survive and be a light of change in the world. He held onto that thought as he and Fred left the car and tried to find a safe spot to spend the day.

As they walked along the streets, Gentil heard singing and was drawn to a nearby Sudanese church.

Before they could go in, a man approached them. Gentil was worried; what would this man want?

"You are not from around here," the man said. "Where are you from?"

It was the question that everyone asked and the one Gentil worried most about. Even though he was away from the worst of the tribal warfare that plagued Rwanda and Congo, Uganda had its own share of troubles. Reports of Uganda's involvement in the second Congo War, and accusations of torture, beatings, and kidnappings for political reasons made Gentil apprehensive about disclosing his background. Would the person be prejudiced against the Banyamulenge tribe? Would there be trouble?

"We are refugees from Congo," he said. "From the region Sud Kivu, but we have lived in Rwanda for the past ten years." He waited to see the man's reaction.

"I know a man from that region," the stranger said after a moment. "You should meet him. Maybe he has news of your village or family."

Gentil and Fred were anxious to feel less alone in this foreign place, but they were also cautious.

"Where is he?" There were parts of the city where Gentil definitely did not feel safe going to.

"He works in the church here."

Gentil and Fred exchanged glances. Surely they would be safe in a church.

"We would be happy to meet him," Gentil said.

The man took them inside the red brick building. It seemed the man from Sud Kivu was busy so Gentil and Fred waited.

The choir was just beginning to practise. Gentil enjoyed sitting in the quiet interior of the church, listening to the singing voices soothe his mind and body. He noticed several musical instruments off to the side, not being used to accompany the singers. There was only one man on the keyboard, but no one on drums or guitars. Gentil looked longingly at the guitars; he missed playing but he was so happy to even see instruments again.

"Hi, my name is Damas. I heard you were looking for me," a man said, coming over after the choir finished practising, "and that you are from Sud Kivu."

"That's right," Gentil said.

"Me as well," he said. "Welcome to our church. We have a good choir, don't you think?"

Gentil and Fred nodded.

Damas waved the choir director over.

"This is Lasu Emmanuel. He is in charge of the music program here."

Lasu smiled at them.

"I saw you looking at the instruments and smiling. That is something a musician would do. Can you play?" Lasu asked Gentil.

"Yes," Gentil said.

"Really? Can you come and play something

for me, then?"

"Sure."

Gentil was a bit nervous because he had never had formal lessons. Also, this was English music and an entirely different style than what he was used to. But because Gentil and Fred had learned to play by ear, not by looking at written music, they began playing the music they had just heard. The choir members were impressed and began to sing along. It was the best Gentil had felt in a long time.

When they got ready to leave, Lasu came over to them.

"You two have talent. Maybe you can come and join us again?"

"We'd love to," Gentil told him.

"Where can I find you?"

Gentil and Fred exchanged glances.

"We don't really have a permanent place yet. We've registered for the camps, but they said it would take time."

Lasu looked shocked.

"So you have nowhere to go?"

They nodded.

"I've been a refugee, too. From Sudan. I know what it is like to leave everything behind and go to a place where you don't know anybody. As long as I have something to do with it, you will have someplace to stay."

He left the room to find the pastor, and when he came back, he was smiling.

"The church owns a room nearby and you are welcome to stay there as long as you need," Lasu said.

Although grateful for the offer, Gentil wanted to compensate the man for his kindness.

"How can we repay you?" he asked.

"Will you play with us in return for your room and board?" the man asked.

Gentil and Fred were thankful they didn't have to hide in an abandoned car anymore. The room was small, but comfortable, and the church arranged for them to get the food they needed at the local store on the church's account. They ended up staying for about three months and spent the time learning to play more songs. The new hymns were different from what Gentil was used to, and he enjoyed the challenge of learning a new style of music.

After three months, Fred and Gentil were contacted by InterAid Uganda and told that they needed to go to a camp outside Kampala called Kyaka II. Gentil was sorry to leave the church, but as refugees, they were required to go.

The camp was a frightening place for the two young men. They felt very much alone. Out of almost 16,000 refugees, only three others were from their tribe. Worse than that, the news soon spread that a camp in Burundi had been attacked and the Banyamulenge there were targeted— more than 160 Banyamulenge refugees had been killed and many more wounded.

They had only been in the camp for about a month when the threats started.

"Hey, Gentil," another refugee called to him one day. "Did you hear what happened in Gatumba?"

Gatumba was the camp in Burundi where the attack happened.

Gentil said nothing.

"When your time comes," the other refugee continued, "I'll be the first to get you. I'll cut your head off."

Gentil was terrified. He told Fred. Fred had been threatened, too.

"We have to get out of here," Fred said. "Tonight."

That evening Fred sold their blanket and tent for whatever they could get for them. They needed money for transportation back to Kampala. They left the few clothes they had brought from the city behind so no one would realize that they were leaving.

They found a man with a small motorcycle called a boda boda. He agreed to take the boys to the main street where they could catch a bus into the city. So the three of them squeezed onto the small motorbike.

The trip took about 45 minutes, but to Fred and Gentil it seemed like hours. People along the road began yelling at them.

"Your nights are numbered, Banyamulenge! Just wait!"

A few miles later someone ran toward the boda boda with a weapon, calling, "Stop! Stop now!"

"No, please don't stop!" Gentil urged the boda boda driver. "Just speed all the way and we will pay you all the money we've got in our pockets."

Luckily the driver did just that and they arrived at the bus stop. After they paid him they took the bus back into Kampala.

The next day they ran into a man they had met in Kampala earlier. They told him about their experience in the camp and how they left in terror.

"Where will you stay?" the man asked.

Gentil and Fred looked at each other and shrugged.

"The church where you were before is struggling for funds. I'm not sure they could take you back. But I am living at a place called AGAPE. It was started by a Catholic priest named Father Francis. They give rooms and meals to refugees who have documents but nowhere to stay."

"That would be wonderful," Gentil said, knowing the dangers that lurked everywhere.

"You can only stay one month, though."

"Anything would be better than a night on the streets," Gentil said.

The following Sunday, Gentil and Fred went to a nearby church to pray. It is customary in Ugandan churches that newcomers stand and introduce themselves. Gentil mentioned that he and Fred were from Congo and that they were musicians.

After the service, the music director asked if they wanted to play something. Gentil jumped at the chance.

Members of the church heard the music and began to dance and sing. Gentil could feel the tears welling in his eyes, just at the chance to play music again.

"Where do you go to church?" the director asked when they were finished.

"We don't have a church yet."

"How much do you charge?" he asked.

Gentil and Fred looked at one another.

"You want us to charge you to play music here?" Gentil asked, shocked. It was a startling question. For Gentil and his family, music was something they did just for the joy of it; they never thought of it as a way to earn a living. The idea that he could pay his way in the world with his music was an astonishing thought for him.

"Well, what we need is someplace to stay while we wait for our family," Gentil said, "and some necessities to live on."

The director asked them to wait a few minutes as he ran to speak with the pastor. He came back and told Gentil and Fred that the church would pay for a small room and their living expenses in return for their musical skills.

It was a fulfilling time for Gentil. He enjoyed improving his technique and expanding his repertoire by playing all day from early morning until the evening. He never got tired of it. Sometimes he played until his hands were so sore he couldn't play anymore.

In December 2004 came a great Christmas gift—with his father safely out of Congo, Gentil's family was able to leave the violence in Rwanda and join him and Fred in Uganda. The room where

Gentil and Fred had been staying was way too small for a family of twelve, so his father found a small house to rent. It had only two rooms and was about an hour's walk away from the church, but at least the family was together again.

Gentil started thinking about taking his music to a new level, to make it more of a career. The idea that music was something he could do to make a living was an exciting prospect. An opportunity to do this arose one day when a man named James Muhairwe listened to him play the keyboard at the church.

After church service one Sunday, he sought Gentil out to speak with him.

"I love the passion you bring to your playing," James said. "You have made me want to get involved more in the music ministry of this church."

"I'm so happy to hear that," Gentil said, smiling.

"I hope they are paying you well. We don't want to lose you."

"They are taking good care of us. They've given me the opportunity to play and I have my family here now."

"No payment? I don't think that's right."

"It's what the church can afford," Gentil told him.

"Then, what can I pay you?" he asked Gentil. "I want to make sure you are properly compensated."

"We're fine," Gentil said.

"There must be something I can offer."

Gentil had seen James at the church before; he knew that the man worked with computers and was familiar with many kinds of software. Cool Edit was the name of a music mixing software that Gentil had heard about. This program could help him produce music, and he desperately wanted to learn how to use it. Knowledge would be better payment than money at this time. There was still so much Gentil wanted to know and do with music.

"You know what? Don't pay me anything," Gentil told him. "Teach me how to use music mixing software. I want to learn to produce music."

"Really? That's it?" the man asked. "Well, the problem is I don't know how to teach; I'm not a teacher. I know the software you would need, but I'm not a musician, either. I'll tell you what. I'm going to show you the basics and give you access to my computer and if you have any software questions, I will answer them for you, but you will have to figure out the music side of things yourself."

Gentil was thrilled and threw himself into this new project. He knew that if he could figure out how to record, mix, and produce, he could really turn music into a career. The drive to do this was stronger than anything he had felt before. Music had saved him when he was at his lowest point: could it now light the way to his future?

To take advantage of this new opportunity, Gentil had to go to the man's office at night, because it was the only time he had access to the computer as the man needed to use it during the day to work. He also knew his parents would be against him walking out on the dangerous streets at night, so he had to sneak out. He would sometimes spend all night there, even giving up sleep completely in order to spend every available moment working on mastering the software.

Two months later, Gentil met a musician from the first church that welcomed him in Uganda who wanted to make a CD. By now, Gentil had good working knowledge of the software and offered to produce this man's music. They both felt that the inspirational songs might help people who had been living with war and conflict to heal.

The CD was a success with more sales than either of them expected. With his newfound wealth, the man came back to find Gentil and told him that he was so good at music production that he needed to build a studio so he could produce music for other musicians.

Gentil couldn't believe what he was hearing—it was the opportunity he had been waiting for. With this man's financial backing, Gentil was able to rent a suitable location and buy the necessary equipment. With the music studio built, Gentil helped produce hundreds of CDs for artists from Sudan, Uganda, and Rwanda. He was making real income from his music even though he was still finishing high school. It was a dream come true... but life had another twist in store for him.

Gentil with his grandfather and siblings (from left to right Gentil, Reagan, grandfather, Mandela, Console):

Courtesy of Gentil Misigaro

Gentil as a child in Rwanda, 1981:

Courtesy of Gentil Misigaro

Top Left: Gentil teaching guitar class at Status4: *Courtesy of Gentil Misigaro*

Top Right: Gentil and his band performing at their CD release party on August 22, 2014: *Credit: Don Windsor*

Middle: Gentil dancing with younger brother David to the song "Beautiful People": *Credit: Don Windsor*

Bottom Right: Gentil in concert with Spirit's Call Choir and the Status4 Children's Choir: *Credit: Don Windsor*

7

Even though Gentil's family was happy to be together, Uganda was far from the peaceful place they had been hoping for.

"Gentil, you have to hurry," Jerome Rutagarama called to him one day as he and one of his younger brothers, Mandela, were walking home. Jerome was one of the pastors at his father's new parish.

"What's wrong?"

"Two men came to the church a few minutes ago asking for your father. They said they were policemen, but I think they looked suspicious. They didn't show any badges or warrants or anything. I'm really worried for your father."

The two brothers raced toward home. As they came close to their neighbourhood they stopped dead in their tracks.

"They have a gun to his head," Mandela whispered.

Gentil didn't believe the two men were

police officers, either. He had heard the stories circulating around Kampala of refugees being captured, tortured, and killed. He was terrified that his father was being targeted so he called the police station on his cell phone and told them he believed his father was being kidnapped by rebels.

Suddenly, Mandela picked up a large rock and ran toward their father and the kidnappers.

"Mandela, get back here!" Gentil said to his brother, but Mandela kept walking.

"Let him go or I'm going to stone your car!" Mandela threatened.

The kidnappers looked around nervously. Mandela's shouts were starting to get attention from the neighbours.

"If you don't move we'll shoot you!" one kidnapper shouted to Mandela.

"Don't shoot my son!" Gentil's father yelled. "I'll go with you."

By now a crowd had gathered. "If you're taking him, I'm coming, too," said one neighbour named Issa Billias. He climbed in beside Gentil's father.

Knowing there were too many witnesses now, the kidnappers drove to the police station where they had some corrupt friends on the force. They bribed the officers to hold Gentil's father without pressing any charges.

For four weeks Gentil travelled daily to the jail to make sure his dad was still alive. It was dangerous though because just by visiting him, Gentil became a target, too. He noticed that he was being followed as he left the jail and had to take a different route to get home than the one he used to go there. He even had to change his clothes along the way to lose the men tailing him. Finally lawyers working with Amnesty International managed to free his father.

Back home safe, there were still daily reports of attacks, robberies, and shootings around Kampala. At night there were home invasions and kidnappings. The family began taking turns sleeping at night, always leaving someone on guard in case of trouble. There seemed to be nowhere they could go to escape the nightmare of fear and violence.

Once again Gentil turned to music. The peace and joy he felt while playing kept him from becoming bitter and angry with his lot in life. Not only had playing piano and guitar with the church provided him with a place to stay and food to eat when he was homeless and starving, but also his music production work was bringing some much needed income to his family.

Gentil never forgot to be grateful for the

blessings he had. Every day he had to walk by the camp on his way to the studio. It moved him to see all the people in that desperate situation he had been lucky enough to escape. When he passed by, he gave them what money he could, but he wanted to do more. He wanted the money he was making from his music not just to help two or three people, or just his family, but to help more people in a bigger way.

He knew that if he were able to get more recognition as a musician, he could then have even more opportunities to make money, and in turn, more opportunities to help others. He also wanted to use the influence of music to change people's way of thinking. He wanted those who felt trapped to feel hope again, and he wanted those in charge to make changes for these people.

Other than playing in the church, Gentil's music was still a personal thing. He produced other musicians' songs but not his own. He saw the lives that other artists touched with their work and he wanted to have that impact, too. Gentil decided he wanted to push himself to perform and to sing, so that he could start to make a difference.

Gentil had no training in voice but once he set his mind to something, there was no stopping him. As he had done with guitar and piano, when it came to singing, Gentil taught himself. He knew he would have to strengthen his voice and its range if he were to sing in front of large crowds, so he went to big empty spaces to practise. Often, he used the empty church at night.

Gentil worked at his singing every night for weeks and pushed his voice so hard that he lost it. He couldn't speak or sing at all. In frustration he gave up any idea of performing as a singer, thinking that it was not meant to be. He would go back to producing other artists and be content with that.

One day he went to the church to practise on the keyboard, thinking he was alone. After resting his voice for a few weeks, it had come back, so as he sat there playing, he began to sing along. Some choir members who had not yet left after their practice heard him and came over.

"Hey, who is that singing?" they asked him.

"That was me," Gentil admitted.

"No! We know you—you don't sing."

"Well, yes I do."

"Even those high notes? Really? You're good!"

Gentil was surprised. He had given up thoughts of singing, but maybe he was wrong. Maybe all his practising and training had worked. A small spark of self-confidence started to grow.

He seized every opportunity he could to sing for groups, big and small.

As Gentil started singing and composing his own music, he realized how much he didn't know. Teaching himself the basics could only take him so far; to really succeed he needed proper training. Now that he had finished high school, he desperately wanted to go to university in Kampala to study music properly but the entrance exam was a big problem. Part of it was an audition where he would have to play a difficult piece of music. All the songs he played were hymns and traditional songs that he had taught himself. None of those would do for an audition piece. He needed help.

Using the ingenuity that had gotten him this far in life, Gentil sought out one of the music professors at the university.

"Excuse me, Professor?"

"Yes. Can I help you?"

"I hope so. I was wondering if you could play this piece of music for me."

The professor took the sheet music from Gentil and studied it.

"You want me to play this?"

"I would really appreciate it."

"Can I ask why?"

"I need to play it for an important performance and I would like to hear it played by a master so I know what to strive for."

Gentil knew this was only a little lie—the real reason was that he couldn't read the music himself and was going to try to play it by ear. He only picked that particular piece because it looked interesting.

The professor played the piece three times for Gentil. By the third time Gentil had it memorized. He practised it over and over, and finally on the day of the audition, he sat down for the admissions panel and played.

When he finished, the panel was quiet. Had he played so badly that they were speechless? Did they know he was self-taught and they would laugh him out of the university?

"What made you pick this piece?" one of the judges asked him.

What could Gentil say—he had just picked it at random.

"I don't know. Why?" he asked. Had he made a huge mistake? Was there something wrong with this piece?

"Well, it happens to be the piece that our students play in their final year of study!"

Gentil was accepted into the program.

***

For two years he had classical training, including keyboard, guitar, voice, music theory, and music history. Music was now his whole life, just as he had hoped.

During this time Gentil's family had regular contact with the United Nations High Commissioner for Refugees (UNHCR). This organization was trying to help them find a permanent place to call home.

After living in Uganda for five years, Gentil and his family were finally called in to the UNHCR office to speak with a caseworker.

"Where are you from?"

There was that question again. Gentil's mother told the story of their troubles in Congo, the threat of attacks, beatings, and killings, and the family's long journey to Rwanda.

"Do you have family still in Congo?" she asked them. "Many of our refugees are able to return home to live with relatives."

"There is no one left," his father told the worker.

"No relatives at all?" she asked.

"No relatives, no friends, no neighbours," he said and told her of the horror of learning that almost the entire village had been killed on Lake Tanganyika and how he thought he had lost his family, too. He told her of his parents who had stayed behind, only to learn that they had also died, and how he was now raising his four younger siblings along with his own six children.

The caseworker frowned. "Well, could you go to another nearby village then, in Sud Kivu?"

"Our tribe, the Banyamulenge, are a people with no home," his father continued. "The Congolese government will not accept us as citizens, and we are targeted for violence in Rwanda."

"Well, how did you come to Uganda?"

It was Gentil's turn to tell how he and Fred had arrived first to escape being forced into the war, how no one would help them, but how they eventually found their way to InterAid to register.

"Which camp are you in?"

"We are not in a camp; we have an apartment here in Kampala. I work for the church."

"What do you do for the church?"

"I am a musician."

"And you?" she asked, pointing to Gentil's father. "What do you do?"

"I am a pastor."

She sighed. "We really have no need for more pastors or church musicians."

There was silence in the room. What would happen to them? Where would they go?

"I think you might be good candidates for emigration. Would you be willing to move to another country?"

Willing to move? That almost made Gentil laugh. All they had done for the past fifteen years was move. Each time they hoped to find peace and stability and a hopeful future, but all they found was more violence, death, and fear.

The family told the worker they would welcome a chance to leave this area. So next came more interviews. This time they were asked more questions: what their strengths were, what skills they had, which languages they spoke, and what their needs were. The caseworker told them that several countries, including Australia, the United Kingdom, the United States, and Canada were offering refugee status to citizens of war-torn countries.

In December 2009 came the news the family had waited so long to hear: they were accepted as refugees and would finally find a peaceful and safe place to call home. They didn't know it at the time—for their own protection, their destination was kept quiet until right before their departure—but the country that would welcome them was Canada.

8

Knowing that they were leaving, but not knowing where they were going, the family prepared to uproot yet again. They told only their closest friends. They had heard stories of emigrating families being attacked or even killed by others who were desperate or jealous of those leaving. The family quietly bought things they might need and gave away other things they would not. Once again the musical instruments had to be left behind. Gentil had to give up his studio and music production business and tell the church that they would need new accompanists.

When the family finally got the news that their new home would be Canada, it made them feel as if they had won the lottery. Canada had a great reputation as a peaceful, prosperous country—so peaceful that some people had even speculated that Canada didn't even have an army!

The UNHCR set up some orientation sessions for Gentil and his family to learn about their soon-to-be new home: the education system, the government system, housing, employment, and of course, the climate.

These sessions only helped to add to their excitement. The possibility of being able to live and work without the constant terror of attacks seemed like a faraway dream. Did such countries really exist?

The last few weeks passed in a blur and before he knew it, Gentil was in a taxi heading to the airport.

"Are you worried about flying?" Fred asked him.

"No. Why?"

"You look scared."

"I'm not afraid of getting on a plane..." Gentil looked out the van window at the people staring at them as they drove by. "...I'm afraid of *not* getting on a plane."

"What do you mean?" Fred asked.

"We are so close now, so close to starting a new life, that I'm worried it won't happen. I'm worried that someone will stop the van and attack us."

Fred looked out the window. "But we've survived so much, and remember, grandfather said we would make it."

Gentil nodded and held on to that thought.

Finally a tall, grey, rectangular building covered in windows came into sight. The vans pulled up to two large sliding-glass doors with a sign overhead that read "Welcome to Entebbe International Airport." People of all sorts were hurrying through the doors, carrying or pulling suitcases.

Gentil and his family got out of the vehicles, grabbed their luggage, which contained the only belongings they had left in the world, and headed into the airport. They checked their luggage and then stood in line for security.

The UNHCR had arranged for the family's travel visas in advance, but because visas are often stolen and sold on the black market, Gentil and his family didn't receive them until this moment at the airport.

For Gentil, it now all finally felt real. He was holding in his hand the document that would allow him and his family to start a new life.

Their first flight was to Amsterdam, the Netherlands. As the plane took off, Gentil looked out the window to watch the trees and roads grow smaller and smaller, and he realized that it was his last glimpse of Africa. When they came back down out of the clouds, he would see a totally different landscape.

Gentil had never flown before but his thoughts on the plane were not about the food or movies on the flight, but how dramatically things in his life were changing. There were eleven members of his family on board: his parents, his five siblings, and his three youngest aunts and uncles. His oldest uncle had stayed behind to start a new life in Kenya. No one spoke much on the flight. They were all thinking about what they were leaving behind and what they were looking forward to in their futures.

The Schiphol Airport in Amsterdam was huge. Their layover was several hours long but no one really had an appetite; it was as if they were all in a state of numbness. The family was relieved to finally board the second flight to Toronto, Canada. Eight hours later Gentil felt the plane start to descend.

"Welcome to Toronto," the pilot's voice said over the loudspeaker.

It was still dark out as they approached the airport.

"Look at all the lights!" Gentil's youngest brother, David, said, pointing out the window. His smile lit up his face.

The rows of lights made grid patterns on the ground and seemed to go on forever.

Gentil looked over at his mother across the aisle. Tears were running down her face.

"Are you okay?" he asked her.

"I'm fine," she said, wiping her cheeks. "I'm just so happy."

"What are you looking forward to the most?" David asked Gentil.

"Not having to take turns sleeping at night."

"Me, too. Or waking up to see some guy trying to break through the window."

The plane touched down and they taxied to the terminal. Landing in Toronto in February 2010 was the first time that Gentil put his feet on the ground of his new homeland.

Immigration personnel met the family at the airport and brought coats, boots, hats, and gloves for each of them, knowing that they couldn't buy these items in Africa before they left. The family was grateful because even walking through the tunnel from the plane to the terminal, they could feel the bite of the cold air. Outside the windows in the waiting area, they could see that Canada, in the middle of winter, looked very different from the country and continent that had been their home until now. The greys and browns were so different from the vibrant colours of Africa.

After their layover in Toronto, they boarded

another plane for the last leg of their journey, which would bring them to their final destination: Winnipeg, Manitoba. If anything, Manitoba looked even colder than Ontario.

In the Arrivals area of the Winnipeg International Airport, the family members claimed their bags and then gathered to find out from their immigration liaison what they were supposed to do now and where they were to go. Two days of travel across nine time zones had left them all exhausted. But Gentil was eager to experience his first winter.

"What do you think snow feels like?" he asked his father, looking out the window. Outside, the sky was grey and the ground was grey and it was hard to see where one ended and the other began.

"I don't know," his father said. "Maybe it's grainy like the sand on the shores of Lake Tanganyika."

"The way it falls, I think it must be soft like feathers," Gentil said.

He wondered, too, what it would feel like to have cold air in his lungs instead of the hot, humid air he was used to.

He wasn't the only one excited to find out. David raced to the exit doors of the airport.

"Wait for us!" Gentil's mother called, but he didn't listen.

David stepped outside. Moments later, his family watched in horror as he stopped short and started choking. His father ran to him and pulled him back inside, trembling.

"What kind of place have we come to?" his mother asked, frightened. "Is the air outside dangerous?"

"Will we all choke when we go outside and start collapsing?" Reagan asked.

Gentil looked around. None of the other people in the airport seemed concerned. People pushed past them laughing and talking and walking through the sliding doors without so much as pausing. He waited to see if they, too, were going to fall over and gasp for air, but they continued on as if nothing were wrong.

"We're going to have to go out there," his father said. "Everyone cover your mouths with your collars or scarves and move slowly."

Gentil stayed near the others, hoping he would be there to catch anyone who started to topple over before their heads hit the concrete sidewalk. Was coming to Canada a good idea after all?

They moved forward slowly, carefully. The door slid open and they stepped outside. Gentil took a careful breath. It was a shock to feel the icy air on his cheeks and down his throat. To his relief, though, no one was choking. Their liaison from Accueil Francophone, the organization that would help them settle, joined them outside and directed them to some waiting vans.

The blast of heat from inside the van was a welcome feeling for Gentil. As they pulled away and headed into town, he got his first look at his new home. Piles of snow lined the roadways and covered the roofs of all the buildings, which had smoke coming out of their chimneys. Trees and shrubs were reduced to black lines against a grey sky. It was going to take some time to get used to winter, but after all they had been through, it was a small thing to overcome—they were home.

The vans drove them into a section of Winnipeg called St. Boniface where the liaison explained there was a large French-speaking community. In fact, it is one of the largest French-speaking communities outside of the province of Quebec. This was reassuring to the older members of the family who knew French.

The vans pulled up to a cluster of homes called transitional housing: two duplexes that the family of eleven could use while finding a permanent place to live. Most immigrant families spend only a few months in transitional housing. Inside, Immigration workers had also provided the essentials for the family to settle in for the night: food, toiletries, and bedding.

That night the family slept without the fear of a nighttime attack, raid, or kidnapping for the first time in fifteen years.

9

"I'm not going."

"Neither am I."

"I don't want to choke again," David said.

No one wanted to go out in the cold to get supplies. Those first few months were difficult for Gentil and his family. While they were thrilled to be in Canada, it was a little overwhelming to try and navigate all the new things at once. The items L'Accueil had left in the house for them were enough to get them by for a few days, but now someone needed to go shopping.

"It's too dangerous," Gentil's mother said.

"But we need to buy some things," Gentil said. "Our liaison told us how to get to the store. I'll do it. It's just a short ride on the bus."

"And what if you get lost?" his mother asked. "You'll freeze to death for sure."

"It can't be that bad—other people are riding the bus today, and going to work or shopping. It won't even take me that long; the lady from

L'Accueil told us the bus route we need."

"I don't like it. I'll worry until you are back safe in this house."

Gentil bundled up in his warmest clothes and his new coat and ventured out. Surely it couldn't be any more difficult than fleeing to Uganda from Rwanda through hostile, landmine-infested, territory, he thought.

The wind pulled at his coat and his fingers became stiff with cold even inside his gloves as he waited for the bus. He knew that he had to take a bus that went downtown, and when he got off he needed to go toward the big sports complex called the MTS Centre, which was impossible to miss, and then turn right onto Portage Avenue. A short walk up Portage and he should be there. It sounded straightforward enough.

He caught the city bus and as he rode along, a mounting sense of panic grew. Gentil realized that the bus wasn't going the way he had been told—he wasn't passing any of the landmarks he had been given. He rang the bell and got off. It was then, wandering the streets of Winnipeg in freezing temperatures, that he understood he was totally and completely lost. Back in Africa, Gentil was used to being able to walk anywhere he needed to go, but this was a whole different story in Canada.

Tall grey buildings channelled the winds down the roads making it hard for Gentil to catch his breath. His eyes watered from the cold as he scanned the street signs looking for anything that sounded familiar.

A guitar store caught his eye. How he wished his errand was shopping for a new guitar! He couldn't stop to dream in front of the window display, though; he needed to find the department store, get the food and supplies he and his family needed, and find his way home before his mother was right and he froze to death.

People pushed past him, hurrying with their heads down to get to their destinations as quickly as possible. He was comforted when he saw the street sign for Portage Avenue, but the street was much larger than he had expected.

"So do I go right or left on Portage now?" he said to himself. "I'm so turned around I don't know which way to go."

He spied the MTS Centre.

"Left, I think. Now how far down the street was it again?"

After a long and exhausting search, he finally found the department store. He stood in the doorway breathing hard. He shopped quickly, grabbing the few things they needed, anxious to get back to their house. First, though, he had to face the journey home.

At the bus stop, he waited on a bench with another man.

"Hey, where are you from?" the man asked. Even in Canada it seemed this was the first question he was asked.

"I'm from Congo," Gentil replied.

"Like, Africa?"

"Yeah, Africa."

"So, must have been tough there, like, with no food or anything."

Gentil was confused. Was that the image the rest of the world had of Africa? That everywhere people were starving and homeless?

"Actually, we ate well," Gentil assured the man. He wasn't sure whether the man was joking or just uninformed.

"Oh. Well, is this the first time you've been to a city?"

"No. I lived for a while in Kampala, Uganda. It is a large city, with over a million people."

A bus came and the man got on it, but the conversation left Gentil a bit uneasy. Would he face discrimination here, like he did in Africa? He was happy to see his bus pull up and this time head in the right direction. He was never so thrilled to see their duplex as on that day. The whole trip left him badly shaken with fright and he vowed not to go out again. Ever. Or at least until it warmed up again.

For a month, Gentil kept his word and stayed in the house, staring out the windows at this foreign world with its uncomfortable climate. But by the end of March he was experiencing what many Canadians call "cabin fever"—that restless, irritable feeling people have when they are shut up indoors for long periods of time.

Gentil was also missing his music—so many times in his life music had helped him get through difficult periods. Perhaps it would help again now. He decided to try going out again, this time with a different purpose: he was going to buy a guitar.

He remembered the guitar store he had seen on Portage Avenue during his disastrous shopping trip. He was sure he could find it again, and besides, buying a guitar was worth the anxiety he felt. This time, the bus went the way he expected and he found the store with little trouble. He made it back safely, and with him was a prized possession—a guitar.

It was freeing for Gentil to play, and the music was once again an outlet for his emotions.

As the weather warmed up, and with a little

more confidence in finding their way around, the family began going to the Centre d'Accueil et d'Établissement (CAÉ).

The Centre had programs and activities that the family could participate in. More importantly, they were able to learn about their new country and its culture in French. While the younger siblings who spent most of their time in English-speaking Uganda were comfortable with English in Winnipeg, Gentil's parents, aunts, and uncles, who had grown up mostly in Congo, preferred French.

The CAÉ offered dance lessons, art shows, French movies, celebrations for St. Jean Baptiste Day, comedy shows, and, of course, music. Jazz nights and music festivals were Gentil's favourite. They gave him a chance to discover the music of his new home; how it was different and how it was the same as the music he knew and loved.

"Hi, my name is Gentil. I am a musician."

This was how Gentil introduced himself. Whether it was at orientation meetings, cultural centre activities, or festivals, it was Gentil's way of trying to make connections in the music world. What better way than to identify himself as a musician?

"So you're a musician?" a man at the Centre said after Gentil's introduction. "Me, too. I'm a drummer. What do you play?"

"Guitar and keyboard."

"Our group could use a guitar player at an event we're doing this weekend. Do you want to come along? We're playing for Amnesty International and you could really help us out."

Gentil jumped at the chance to play again, especially because this event was being held to aid the tsunami victims after the disaster in South Asia only a couple of months prior. When the day arrived, he went to the hall where they were going to perform and waited in an area downstairs. One of the organizers came over to him. She was looking for a singer on the schedule. He was nowhere to be found and there was now a hole in the program.

"Who are you?" the organizer asked Gentil.

"Gentil Misigaro."

She scanned her sheets. "Are you here to sing?"

"No, I'm playing guitar."

"Do you sing?"

"Yes."

"Great. Would you perform a song for us?"

Gentil had nothing prepared, but that was only a small problem to someone who had played by ear and composed his own songs for so long.

He also did not want to miss an opportunity to perform.

"Sure."

On the spot Gentil composed a song commemorating the victims of the tsunami and minutes later performed it for the crowd. It felt so good to play and sing again, and he felt alive in the moment. Afterwards he received a rousing ovation with requests for an encore. Coming off the stage, he nearly bumped into a man with his hand extended for a handshake.

"Hi, my name is Terry MacLeod. I really enjoyed your performance. The way you play guitar with your teeth when you get carried away is really something else!"

"Thank you," Gentil said, "It felt good to play my music in front of people again."

"Again?"

"I've just recently moved to Canada from Congo. I'm trying to re-start my music career here."

"Well, I just might be able to help with that. I work for the CBC—the Canadian Broadcasting Corporation. Would you be up for an interview?"

Gentil was thrilled to bring his story and talent to the attention of more people. After the interview he was invited to play at another musical event in Winnipeg's Central Park.

Once again, Gentil was a hit and that event led to another and then another. Gentil's reputation as a musician started to grow.

Just as music had healed him and opened doors for him in Africa, music was helping Gentil build a bridge to his new home. It was a good start, but maybe, he thought, his music could do much more.

10

E ven though Gentil's situation had improved dramatically over the last year, he never forgot what it was like to struggle through life. He saw in his new community that some people were struggling in a different way: they were dealing with physical and mental disabilities. Gentil could relate to living a life full of challenges, but he wanted to understand how they dealt with theirs.

Back in Africa, there weren't programs available to help these most vulnerable citizens. The effect of years of warfare can leave countries with no infrastructure, money, or resources to care for people with special needs. They are left to navigate the world with no support. Gentil was happy to see that there were programs and opportunities in Canada for these children and adults to learn, grow, and participate in their community.

He heard of a not-for-profit organization called St. Amant that dedicates itself to providing care, education, and support for those living with special needs in Manitoba. Gentil was pleased to see how much could be done to improve their lives. He wanted to help. He applied for a position there and was accepted. After a training session he began his new job as a support worker.

Gentil wasn't sure what to expect. At first he simply helped with the day-to-day care of kids in the program. As he spent more time with these children, Gentil noticed a natural musicality in some of them. He wondered if music could be a healing tonic for them, as it had been for him.

Gentil started to supplement the children's regular care with activities that gave them opportunities to explore music. He began with voice lessons, giving them a chance to try singing alone or in a group. Some children surprised him with their ability to repeat a tune they had just heard. Some even wrote their own songs.

As time went on, some showed an interest in music production and were thrilled to join Gentil in a recording studio and go through the steps to record their own work. The pride in their accomplishments when they listened to themselves sing and play on a recording was infectious. Gentil was inspired to get back to writing his own songs. Sometimes he would work on them while at the Centre, with the kids around him providing motivation and insight.

One day, Gentil was at the piano at the Centre, playing part of a new song he was composing. A boy who was visually impaired was nearby. During their music activities, this boy had astounded Gentil with his ability to play piano by touch. Often, when one of the five senses is damaged, another sense is strengthened. Blind children are 4,000 times more likely to have perfect pitch.

"It would sound better with a different note," the boy said.

"Which note?" Gentil asked, replaying the line of music.

"At the end, it should go like this." The boy hummed the note he heard in his head.

Gentil found the note on the piano and played the line with the new ending. The boy was right. It was better; in fact, this change took the song in a whole new direction.

It was a reminder to Gentil that music is a universal language that can touch and be understood by all kinds of people, and that language, culture, and even disabilities are not barriers where music is concerned.

Gentil found that his time working with these kids went beyond his expectations. Before he started, he imagined that he would probably stay a few months in the job—it seemed so daunting. Two years later, Gentil was still involved with the kids of St. Amant. He performed shows for them and let the compassion he felt and saw when working with them seep into his music. They constantly surprised and amazed him with their hopeful attitudes and hard work ethic. He thought that when he took the job, it would be all about him helping them. Now he realized that they were helping him, too.

It was around this time that Gentil released his first EP (extended play) CD. He was eager to resume the music production work he was so successful in back in Uganda. Inspiration and hope were all around him, and he wanted to express this through the medium he knew best—his music. He even hoped to eventually do some benefit concerts to help St. Amant. But how could he find the resources to achieve this? Renting a studio would cost money—money Gentil didn't have.

Gentil reached out to the Canadian Centre for Refugee Employment (CCRE). Its mandate is to help promote and provide employment opportunities for war-affected refugees. Maybe they could help him?

There he met Serge Kaptegaine, another

refugee from Congo, who helped him to find funding for recording studio time. Through the CCRE, Gentil connected with other artists. They decided to form their own group, which they called EXILE.Z, the "last exile." The group was composed of musicians of different ethnic backgrounds who wanted to share a message of positivity through their songs. Some of Gentil's siblings also got involved and joined the group or filled in when other members couldn't make performances. These artists also wanted to help others in a more concrete way by donating the proceeds from the sale of the EP to various charities around the country.

Gentil and Serge collaborated on writing the set of six original songs for the EP called *A Better Home*, including titles such as "Canada to My Child," "Manitoba," and "Refugees." The lyrics were heartfelt and spoke of the immigrant experience of coming to a new country and the gratitude of having the chance to forge a new future.

***

"Somebody give me hope of freedom and justice, let me know if I can breathe again."

"I believe in each of us. We can do it, we can make it."

Their music blended traditional African and Western styles with a bit of R&B mixed in for a new sound that reflected the diversity of the group as well as the diversity of their new homeland. The group wanted to dedicate the EP to the "First Nations, seniors, and earlier generations of Canadians who worked and continue working tirelessly to build this beautiful country."

EXILE.Z performed at different events in and around Winnipeg, including the Gratitude Gala. This annual gala evening honours those who improve opportunities for new Canadians and also honours newcomers for their positive contributions to the province. The event includes a formal dinner, awards ceremony, and a keynote speaker, with proceeds from ticket sales going to help former refugees find employment in Manitoba.

At the Gratitude Gala in 2011, Gentil was also an award recipient when he was presented with the Nyota Award. This award is given to a refugee who has made an outstanding contribution or significant achievement in academics, arts and culture, sports, community or volunteer activities. Gentil's work with St. Amant as well as his determination to bring a message of hope and love through his music earned him this honour.

"Receiving the Nyota Award made me realize that my message was getting through to people. It's very inspiring and gratifying to know that our involvement is acknowledged," Gentil said at the gala.

The release of the EP and winning the Nyota Award also renewed Gentil's drive to write, record, and perform. But he wanted to take things further; he wanted to make his music into a career that could change the world.

11

"**D**o you have anything else?" Kevin Gibson asked his friend and music producer, Paul Katsnelson, who was playing demos from local musicians.

"You've heard practically every musician in town," Paul said, "but I do have one song here from this guy from Africa that I met about a year ago."

Paul played the song and Kevin smiled. "That's it. *That's* the sound I want. Who is he?"

"His name is Gentil Misigaro."

Kevin Gibson was a police officer on a mission. After years of seeing and dealing with hundreds of kids who were falling through the cracks in society, he decided to do something about it. He had the idea to start an organization that would provide music and arts programs to under-served and at-risk youth. He believed that young people in Winnipeg could find support and hope through these outlets. As a vocalist and guitar player himself, he knew the power music had to inspire.

Kevin wanted to launch his new organization with a song—a song sung by a local artist. He had been listening to several recordings, but none of them sounded right. Until he heard Gentil.

Kevin met with Gentil and they quickly realized that they had similar views and goals. Gentil was thrilled to be asked to join the team working on Status4, the name Kevin gave to his project (to the emergency responders in Winnipeg, Status4 means "on the scene"). Gentil wanted to help bring Kevin's vision to life; after all, it embodied everything he believed, too: the importance of music as a way to reach, teach, and support people.

Gentil worked with Kevin to develop the music programs that Status4 would offer to kids. These included voice, rhythm, guitar, keyboard, and recording. In the guitar and keyboard classes, students would learn both to play by ear and to read written music. Status4 would provide students with the instruments, music stands, and sound systems they would need.

In voice lessons, not only would participants work on vocal skills but they would also have opportunities to perform at various events in the community. Students interested in music production would start by practising songwriting and then move on to learn about the latest recording technology and devices. In this way, they would apply the skills they learned by recording their own music. The program also offered Tae Kwon Do martial arts training to improve kids' self-esteem, confidence, and self-discipline.

As director of music programs, Gentil was at Status4 almost every day of the week. Programs were held in part of the East End Cultural Centre, an old community centre. With the help of friends and local businesses, Kevin renovated and transformed the building into a music and arts studio.

As he worked there, Gentil started noticing that some of the kids were there almost as often as he was.

"You don't have to take every class," Gentil told one boy with a smile. "You can just pick one or two."

"But I want to come every day," the boy told him. "I love all the classes, and I'm hoping this year to do some recording in the studio with you."

"But with your homework and other activities, isn't it too much?"

"No. I just love being here."

That was a sentiment he heard over and over again. Gentil began to realize that for some of the kids, this program was more than just a place to learn new skills—it was a safe haven, a reason to stay off the streets and out of trouble.

It had another positive effect on some of the kids.

One boy, whom Gentil knew had a lot of musical talent, started acting out in classes. During singing practice, he would disrupt the class by talking out of turn, scraping chairs across the floor, and slamming doors. Gentil encouraged the others to focus on their singing and try to ignore the noise, but it made the class difficult.

Afterwards, Gentil sought out the young man and sat him down to talk.

"Tell me what's going on with you."

The boy was defensive at first. "I'm not doing anything!"

"You seemed to be upset today. It's a shame because you're really good in that class."

At this, the boy looked up. "Do you really think so?"

Gentil nodded. "You have talent. I've always thought so, but when you act out, you aren't using your time to improve."

The look on the boy's face told Gentil that he was surprised by this.

"You...you think I'm good?" the boy asked.

"Yes, very good."

The boy looked visibly upset. After waiting a few moments, he said quietly, "No one has ever told me I was good at anything before. At home, I'm always the bad one, the one in trouble, the 'good for nothing.'"

It was a turning point for the boy. Knowing that someone believed in him changed his behaviour. He settled down and started to really try in class. Gentil couldn't believe it was the same boy, so remarkable was his transformation.

Gentil threw himself into his work, and his responsibilities at Status4 filled his evenings, but he knew he needed to earn a living as well. Gentil began giving private music lessons and also teaching music at a local high school during the day. As well as giving him money to help with the family expenses, it was another opportunity to interact with students. Every music lesson and conversation with his students reminded Gentil that there are ideas and themes that are common around the world. Regardless of their backgrounds or personal stories, people everywhere need hope and love to navigate life's challenges. Gentil knew that music could make a difference.

Students both in the high school and in the Status4 programs shared with Gentil stories of being bullied. They felt targeted all the time, but once they began talking about their experiences playing instruments or using recording equipment, their peers treated them differently. They weren't picked on as often and their self-confidence soared.

That confidence allowed these kids to do things that they might have found too intimidating only a few months previous. One opportunity that came along for the kids at Status4 was the chance to sing at the annual Juno Awards, which were being held in Winnipeg, to honour the best in Canadian music.

"I can't believe we're singing at the Junos!" one of Gentil's students said to him.

"Are we going to be on stage?" another girl asked.

"No," Gentil said. "We've been asked to sing in the Green Room."

"What's a Green Room?" she asked.

"It's the room backstage where the performers wait to go on stage."

"Will we see famous people there?" a boy chimed in.

"Yes," Gentil said. "And you're going to entertain them."

"What songs are we going to sing?"

"Here's a list of the ones I want us to practise. I thought we'd start with 'Imagine' by John Lennon, 'We Are The World,' and the song Laura Jane, Mark Debrincat, Kevin Gibson, and I wrote together: '2 Plus 9.'"

"What about the song we wrote in Songwriting Class?" another girl asked.

Gentil smiled. "Yes, we are going to sing 'Believe,' too."

A big cheer went up from the group.

It was an amazing experience for the kids, and Gentil saw their enthusiasm and dedication through the many hours of rehearsals and performances. He realized that Status4 was more than just an after-school program—it was changing their futures. Some of the young people talked about making music and the arts their careers.

Being with Status4 since its beginning allowed Gentil to see how one person's vision could change the lives of people forever. Gentil began to think of his own imprint on his community and how he could do more.

The idea of making a better world through music changed from just a thought to a plan over the Christmas holidays in 2012. Gentil was called to fill in for a support worker at St. Amant who was sick. As a casual worker, Gentil would come in whenever they needed extra help. He worked there all day, celebrating the season with program participants. When his shift ended, he was tired and eager to get home and spend some time with his own family, but a phone call from a supervisor brought bad news—they couldn't find anyone to come in to replace him. Could he stay for the overnight shift? There were over two hundred residents, and support workers were needed around the clock.

Reluctantly Gentil agreed. Although he was tired, it wasn't the kids' fault that everyone was sick. He settled in for the night. The next morning the news was no better—even more employees were sick. Could he stay?

By the next evening, Gentil was exhausted and upset. *How did I get stuck doing shift after shift?* he wondered, feeling a little sorry for himself.

But as he sat quietly in an armchair, facing another night shift, his thinking changed.

"Every challenge is an opportunity," he said to himself. "What have you been put on this Earth to do?"

He remembered what his grandfather had told him before he left Congo, and knowing that big things were expected of him, he pulled out a notepad and started jotting down notes on what he wanted to do with his life. The thoughts flowed freely until he had several pages filled with ideas. One thing was clear—he wanted to leave the world a better place than what it was. He had seen so much tragedy, so much sadness, so much despair. Surely this wasn't the way the world should work. He hoped to live in a world where people helped and supported each other—where compassion and understanding were the main motivators, not hate and fear.

"How will I accomplish that?" he asked himself. "How can one person make a difference?"

The answer seemed obvious: with his music. That was the gift he had been given—that was the gift he would use.

He listed the different ways he could reach out to people with his music. First, he could use his songs to inform people of what was going on in the world. Information and understanding of other cultures and ideas could bring more compassion for situations that we might not be aware of. Gentil knew firsthand how conflict and war are propagated by hate being passed down from generation to generation. If people realized this, maybe they would break the cycle of violence. Maybe others would be moved to provide relief or volunteer.

He also felt that people who had been victims of violence and difficulties in life could be helped with messages of hope and inspiration. Gentil believed his optimism and positivity could be an example for others—if he could live through loss and desperation, maybe they could find a way to thrive even in difficult situations.

And while encouragement and faith were powerful healers, people needed more tangible things in life, too. Starvation, illness, and ignorance would only fuel the fires of conflict and revolution. People needed food, shelter, medicine, and education in order to once again take control of their lives, communities, and countries. Those things cost money. Gentil knew that the proceeds from any work he did, or any funds he raised, would make a difference in the lives of people around the world. Certainly the money was desperately needed in Africa, but his work at St. Amant showed him that donations in his new country were important, too.

But a movement to change things would be a huge undertaking and he knew that he couldn't do it alone—a better world would need the participation of everyone.

Gentil knew that a tide could change with just a drop of water, and that big changes happened from small acts. If each person around the world performed small acts of kindness, changed their attitudes, or showed love and hope to people around them, those changes would impact outward, like ripples on a pond when a stone is thrown in the still water.

When he was finally able to go home again, his fatigue disappeared and he was full of energy. With the inspiration found in the pages of his notebook, Gentil put his vision into motion and started a non-profit organization he called A Better World Movement. He wanted it to be a way for kids to use music and the arts to express messages of social responsibility.

Gentil began building momentum for the

project by speaking to students at schools all around the city, telling his story and getting them excited about the possibilities and opportunities they have to improve their homes, their schools, their communities, their country, and their world. His main goal is to educate children by showing them that by combining strengths, we can make everywhere better.

"We all go through different situations in our lives, we have different things to offer. You see things around you, in your community or country, and who better than you to change them? Do something about it," he would tell them.

Students were eager to participate and came up with their own ideas of what they could do. Gentil saw his role as helping to arrange opportunities for them to implement their plans to set change into motion. He would lend a hand, whether it was arranging events or helping them book recording time at a studio.

For his part, Gentil looked for opportunities in his own life to make a better world. On his birthday he wanted to do something special, something more than receiving presents. He wanted to use the day to give something to those who had less, especially the children he knew were struggling back in Congo. Giving and sharing are beliefs that have their roots in the culture he grew up in.

Gentil had contact with a friend in Congo who risked his safety to go back and work in the villages near where Gentil grew up. Gentil learned through him that due to killings and sickness, many children there are orphans or are being raised by poor, elderly relatives. These children have none of the opportunities that Gentil, his siblings, and his neighbours and friends in his new home enjoy. Gentil remembered what it was like to be frightened and without hope, especially concerning education.

In the Democratic Republic of Congo, like many African countries, school is not free. Poor families cannot afford to give their children or grandchildren an education—the one thing that can offer them the hope of a better future. And even where schools have no official fees, money for uniforms and supplies can be impossible to obtain.

Gentil knew the value of education, especially in a country that was struggling with the poverty and uncertainty that wars bring. He knew that the chance to go to school would not only give them hope of someday getting a decent job and a steady income, but could also stem the violence that comes from ignorance.

Gentil saw his birthday as an opportunity to help, so that October he hosted a large fundraiser. He was joined by other artists in Winnipeg, and even some of his private students, for this worthy cause. After the event there was also a big dance party on the dance floor, which made it a wonderful night of celebration. The money raised went directly to his friend in Congo to sponsor children in the surrounding villages to go to school.

"Here," Reagan said, handing his brother some bills. "Add this to your fund."

Gentil was astonished to count out $50.00.

"But, isn't this your Christmas money?" he asked "Weren't you going to buy yourself something with it?"

"I was, but I think those kids need school more than I need another game. I see what you're doing every day to help others, and I want to be part of that, too."

Three of his other siblings came forward with their holiday money, too. Gentil was overwhelmed by their generosity and excited to think what that $200 would provide for kids in the small villages that dotted rural Congo.

Gentil made it an annual event. The first year, twenty youngsters were able to go to school. The next year, thirty. The third year, Gentil raised enough money for fifty young students to attend school.

Each year, Gentil looked forward to his birthday event, knowing how much the money made a difference in the lives of those children.

13

Gentil has big plans for the future. He is scaling back on some of his teaching and volunteering in order to spend more time composing and performing. He hopes to be a performer on a much bigger scale because he knows that the more people he can reach, the more people he can help. His sound is a different style of music: a mix of who he is and where he has been. And his message is simple: "Look, I went through all of this and came out the other side; you can, too."

Even today, music is still a refuge for Gentil. When he listens to the news, especially stories from his home country, and hears about killings and kidnappings and tragedies, he goes into his studio and plays. He plays and practises until his spirit is renewed.

Sometimes, when things are so hard that he can't bring himself to play, he listens to the music of other artists, songs that reflect what he is feeling at that moment, and this also helps heal and comfort him. Gentil hopes that his songs do the same for others.

"Stay Strong" is the title song on his latest EP of the same name that was released in August 2014. He wanted the songs on this album to reflect his passion for giving help, hope, and inspiration to others.

The song "Stay Strong" holds special meaning for Gentil, because it is a reflection of the journey he has made so far.

STAY STRONG

Stay strong no matter what you face
know that all days are not the same
tomorrow is a brighter day
no matter what comes your way just
remember
the journey ahead, is shorter
than the mountains you climbed.
Stay strong, stay strong, don't give up,
you're on the edge of the mountain.

Chorus:
I can see the stars gathering
to lift you to a higher sky
I can see the light coming
to brighten your future
and wash away your past
ohohohohohohohohoh

You've come a long way
you've been through a lot
all the battles you may face, your goal
is to win but not to give up.
I've come to tell you this,
through patience, courage, and sticking to what
you believe
you can make it.
Stay strong, stay strong

Bridge:
If you think you can or can't, you are right
if you believe that you can or you can't, you're
right
if someone can fly without wings and reach to
the sky,
if you have courage to carry on, you can make,
you gonna make it

Gentil decided the best way to celebrate his first solo album was to plan a release with a live concert. Friday, August 22nd found Gentil doing what he loves best: being on stage, entertaining people with his music. The launch of his EP was a huge success. After the concert, many people came up to speak with Gentil.

"Your music speaks to my heart," a woman told him. "I didn't want the concert to end."

"You know," another man said, "that was the best concert I've ever been to. This is a show you never forget."

Gentil was thrilled that his music seemed to be touching people and making them feel what he intended—hope, happiness, and love. He couldn't ask for a better outcome, and was excited to sell out of the first printing of his CD in less than two weeks.

That summer was special to Gentil for another reason: he was honoured to be named as one of Canada's Top 25 Immigrants for 2014. This award is given annually to "recognize inspirational immigrants who have come to Canada, achieved success and made a positive difference living here." Gentil, like the other award winners, was recognized as a positive role model for other immigrants who have made their new home a better place to live. Few people have accomplished as much as he has in so short a time; from producing albums, teaching, songwriting, and performing, to devoting so much time to volunteering and even starting his own non-profit organization, A Better World Movement.

Gentil has already performed in major centres across Canada such as Montreal, Toronto, Ottawa, and Calgary. He hopes to bring his music to even more cities in the near future. His eyes are firmly set on what he wants to accomplish and he has the determination to get there.

"I am on the path that my grandfather saw for me, and I am so happy doing what I do."

Gentil's Travels Within Africa

1. Congo

2. Rwanda

3. Congo

4. Uganda

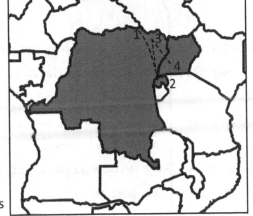

5. Amsterdam,
the Netherlands

6. Toronto, ON

7. Winnipeg, MB

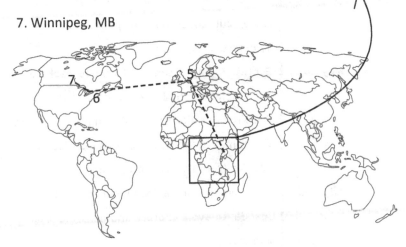

Gentil's Route to Canada ✈

Timeline

October 1988	Gentil is born in Magunga, Sud Kivu, Zaire.
April–July 1994	The genocide in Rwanda kills an estimated 500,000 to 1,000,0000 Rwandans.
October 1994	Gentil, his mother, uncle, and brother flee their village for Rwanda.
October 1996 - May 1997	The First Congo War erupts and brings in a new government.
August 1998 - July 2003	The Second Congo War is fought and when it is over, a new unified government is in place, but thousands of people are left homeless, sick, and starving.
May 2004	Gentil's family attempts to move back to its homeland in Sud Kivu, Congo.
June 2004	The Kivu Conflict erupts in Congo. The family flees back to Rwanda, fearing attacks from the Congolese army.
July 2004	Gentil and his uncle Fred head to Kampala, Uganda, to avoid capture and enlistment as soldiers.
December 2004	Gentil's family joins him in Uganda.
December 2009	Gentil and his family are accepted as refugees to Canada.

February 2010	The family arrives in Winnipeg, Manitoba.
June 2010	Gentil wins the Nyota Award.
April 2011	Gentil and the group EXILE.Z release their EP titled *A Better Home*.
Spring 2011	Status4 opens its doors to under-serviced and at-risk youth in Winnipeg.
Spring 2013	Gentil launches his non-profit organization, A Better World.
June 2014	Gentil is named one of Canada's Top 25 Immigrants for 2014.
August 2014	Gentil releases his first solo EP, *Stay Strong*.

Resources

More about Gentil

Gentil's website: www.gentil.ca

Gentil's YouTube account:
www.youtube.com/user/gentilmis?spfreload=10

Gentil's concert in 2012:
www.bytesizeimages.net/GentilMis/2012/CCFM/
IOS.html

Status4
www.status4.ca

More about the Conflicts in Africa

Books:
Combres, Elisabeth. Broken Memory: *A Novel of Rwanda*. Groundwood, 2009.

Diebert, Michael. *The Democratic Republic of Congo: Between Hope and Despair*. Zed Books, 2013.

Jansen, Hanna. *Over a Thousand Hills I Walk With You*. Carolrhoda Books, 2006.

Stearns, Jason. *Dancing in the Glory of Monsters: The Collapse of the Congo and the Great War of Africa.* PublicAffairs, 2012.

Twagilimana, Aimable. *Hutu and Tutsi.* Rosen Pub. Group, 1997.

Websites:
The BBC answers questions about the conflict in Congo:
www.bbc.com/news/world-africa-11108589

Fact Monster gives readers a brief history of the many changes in Congo's government and the conflicts that arose from them:
www.factmonster.com/ipka/A0198161.html

A timeline of the Democratic Republic of Congo:
www.bbc.com/news/world-africa-13286306

Suroosh Alvi takes viewers on a tour to learn about conflict minerals and rebels in Congo:
www.youtube.com/watch?v=kYqrflGpTRE

How Kids Can Help

A Better World Movement:
www.abetterworldmovement.com

Katimavik: its mission is to prepare youth to become responsible citizens who make positive change in their lives and communities:
www.katimavik.org

Kids Help Phone is a 24/7 counselling and information service for young people. Youth can volunteer to fundraise or help out at events:
www.org.kidshelpphone.ca/get-involved/volunteer/

Teens, adults, seniors, and even schools can volunteer at St. Amant to assist clients living at River Road Place in Winnipeg, Manitoba. Visit its website to find out how:
www.stamant.ca/volunteering/

Canada World Youth provides a variety of programs, in over 20 countries around the world, for youth between the ages of 15 and 35 looking to gain leadership experience through participation in community-driven development projects:
www.canadaworldyouth.org

The International Youth Internship Program
through the Government of Canada gives youth
the opportunity to participate in international
development work:
www.international.gc.ca/development-
developpement/partners-partenaires/iyip-psij/
index.aspx

Index

Acknowledgements

Special thanks to:

Gentil Misigaro, for being so generous with his story and his time and never complaining about my endless lists of questions.

My editors, Solange Messier and Christie Harkin, for making this process a delight with their enthusiasm, talent, and sense of humour.

My brother, Sheldon Rose, for the enormous patience he had explaining musical terms and processes to a non-musical person (me!).

Alex, Chelsey, Nathan, and Haley, who gave me the time to write, the quiet to do interviews, feedback as my first readers, and never-ending belief in me.

My husband, Craig, who is caring enough to know when to ask how my book is coming along and wise enough to know when not to ask.